BEER
IS BETTER THAN WOMEN BECAUSE...
PART II

Written By:
**M.L. Brooks, Donna E. Hanbery, Ivor Matz,
Tam and Craig Westover, and Herbert Kavet**
Illustrated By:
Martin Riskin

© 1993
by **Ivory Tower Publishing Company, Inc.**
All Rights Reserved

Manufactured in the United States of America

30 29 28 27 26 25 24 23 22 21 20 19 18 17 16 15 14 13 12 11 10 9 8 7 6 5 4 3 2 1

Ivory Tower Publishing Co., Inc.
125 Walnut St., P.O. Box 9132, Watertown, MA 02272-9132
Telephone #: (617) 923-1111   Fax #: (617) 923-8839

BEER
IS BETTER THAN WOMEN BECAUSE...

If you shake up a beer it may fizz a little, but will rarely call its mother.

BEER
IS
BETTER
THAN
WOMEN
BECAUSE...

You can bring a beer on a fishing trip without having to listen to it bitch about the mosquitoes.

**BEER
IS
BETTER
THAN
WOMEN
BECAUSE...**

A beer never wants to stay up afterwards talking about respect.

BEER IS BETTER THAN WOMEN BECAUSE...

You can get a fresh new beer no matter how old you are.

BEER
IS
BETTER
THAN
WOMEN
BECAUSE...

If you change your mind about a beer, you don't have to spend the rest of your evening with it.

BEER
IS
BETTER
THAN
WOMEN
BECAUSE...

A beer doesn't change its mind after you've taken off its top.

BEER
IS
BETTER
THAN
WOMEN
BECAUSE...

You don't have to drive a beer home at 3 o'clock in the morning.

BEER
IS
BETTER
THAN
WOMEN
BECAUSE...

You don't have to explain ten times to a beer why going to a nude beach is a better idea than going to the opera.

BEER
IS
BETTER
THAN
WOMEN
BECAUSE...

A beer will never complain if you can't finish it.

BEER
IS
BETTER
THAN
WOMEN
BECAUSE...

You can't get thrown in jail for having a beer
under the grandstands at half-time.

BEER
IS
BETTER
THAN
WOMEN
BECAUSE...

After several beers, you can roll over and go to sleep without having to talk about love.

BEER
IS
BETTER
THAN
WOMEN
BECAUSE...

A beer doesn't initiate sexual harassment suits if you accidently touch their cans.

BEER
IS
BETTER
THAN
WOMEN
BECAUSE...

A beer would never prefer a romantic classic to a good X-rated flick.

BEER
IS
BETTER
THAN
WOMEN
BECAUSE...

A beer doesn't expect flowers and an expensive dinner
before opening up.

BEER
IS
BETTER
THAN
WOMEN
BECAUSE...

A beer likes the way your breath smells in the morning.

BEER
IS
BETTER
THAN
WOMEN
BECAUSE...

A beer never bugs you to have little beers.

BEER
IS
BETTER
THAN
WOMEN
BECAUSE...

You can try dark beers and lite beers without upsetting your parents.

BEER
IS
BETTER
THAN
WOMEN
BECAUSE...

You can share a beer with your friends and they are likely to share theirs with you.

BEER IS BETTER THAN WOMEN BECAUSE...

A beer won't beat you at Scrabble or do your crossword puzzles in ink.

BEER
IS
BETTER
THAN
WOMEN
BECAUSE...

**A beer doesn't make you feel inadequate
if you can't get it opened.**

BEER
IS
BETTER
THAN
WOMEN
BECAUSE...

A beer doesn't expect an hour of foreplay before satisfying you.

BEER
IS
BETTER
THAN
WOMEN
BECAUSE...

A beer doesn't smoke or mind if you smoke, or bug you to shave, workout or fix their car.

BEER IS BETTER THAN WOMEN BECAUSE...

A beer is easy to pick up no matter how late it is.

BEER
IS
BETTER
THAN
WOMEN
BECAUSE...

If your preference to a type of beer or size of beer changes, you don't have to get involved with lawyers.

BEER
IS BETTER THAN WOMEN BECAUSE...

You can try exotic foreign beers without having neighbors worry about property values.

BEER
IS
BETTER
THAN
WOMEN
BECAUSE...

You can pop a beer exactly at the moment you choose.

BEER
IS
BETTER
THAN
WOMEN
BECAUSE...

A beer will never get moody at certain times of the month.

BEER
IS
BETTER
THAN
WOMEN
BECAUSE...

You can have two beers in a row and still have enough energy left for 18 holes of golf.

BEER
IS
BETTER
THAN
WOMEN
BECAUSE...

A beer tastes good after three hours of tennis.

BEER
IS
BETTER
THAN
WOMEN
BECAUSE...

A beer will never bitch about foreplay, afterplay, or doing it too fast or too slow. A beer is always ready when you are.

BEER
IS
BETTER
THAN
WOMEN
BECAUSE...

A beer never complains about the kind of games you play with them.

BEER
IS
BETTER
THAN
WOMEN
BECAUSE...

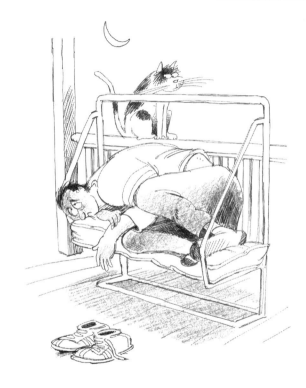

A beer doesn't make you sleep on the couch after you've taken six other beers on a picnic.

BEER IS BETTER THAN WOMEN BECAUSE...

A beer won't slap you in the face for putting it between your legs at a drive-in movie.

BEER
IS
BETTER
THAN
WOMEN
BECAUSE...

A beer always comes in a shape that will fill your hand.

BEER
IS
BETTER
THAN
WOMEN
BECAUSE...

A beer really doesn't care if it's the first, second, or last beer you're enjoying.

BEER
IS
BETTER
THAN
WOMEN
BECAUSE...

After you've put your lips to a beer, a beer never says:
"What are you doing?"

BEER
IS
BETTER
THAN
WOMEN
BECAUSE...

Finishing a beer in three seconds is something to be proud of.

BEER
IS
BETTER
THAN
WOMEN
BECAUSE...

A beer is made from pure ingredients like grain, hops, malt and water. It's not a hodge-podge of perfume, powder, cellulite, and hair spray all held together by control-top pantyhose.

BEER
IS
BETTER
THAN
WOMEN
BECAUSE...

Foreign beers are basically the same as domestic ones.

BEER
IS
BETTER
THAN
WOMEN
BECAUSE...

Before you have a beer, you don't have to spend the evening pretending to be sensitive.

BEER
IS
BETTER
THAN
WOMEN
BECAUSE...

Beers don't complain about being fondled.

BEER
IS
BETTER
THAN
WOMEN
BECAUSE...

You can always get some sort of head with a beer.

BEER
IS
BETTER
THAN
WOMEN
BECAUSE...

You have a pretty good idea of the size of a beer
even before you open it.

BEER
IS
BETTER
THAN
WOMEN
BECAUSE...

You can have a beer on your lunch hour.

BEER
IS
BETTER
THAN
WOMEN
BECAUSE...

A beer looks as good in the morning as it did when the bar closed.

BEER
IS
BETTER
THAN
WOMEN
BECAUSE...

A beer is usually mildly antiseptic, and you won't get any diseases putting your mouth on it.

BEER
IS
BETTER
THAN
WOMEN
BECAUSE...

A beer doesn't fart under the covers and then say it didn't.

BEER
**IS
BETTER
THAN
WOMEN
BECAUSE...**

A beer doesn't notice if you're inexperienced.

BEER
IS
BETTER
THAN
WOMEN
BECAUSE...

A beer can wait until half-time.

BEER
IS
BETTER
THAN
WOMEN
BECAUSE...

A beer knows it's not the size of the container that matters, but how many times you can fill it.

BEER
IS
BETTER
THAN
WOMEN
BECAUSE...

A beer will never tell you to pick up a box of Tampax.

BEER
IS
BETTER
THAN
WOMEN
BECAUSE...

A beer will never turn your den into a sewing room, your bathroom into a laundry room, or your bedroom into a beauty parlor.

BEER
IS
BETTER
THAN
WOMEN
BECAUSE...

A beer rarely keeps pets.

BEER
IS
BETTER
THAN
WOMEN
BECAUSE...

A beer won't clip coupons out of the paper before you've read it.

BEER
IS
BETTER
THAN
WOMEN
BECAUSE...

A beer will never switch channels from "All Star Wrestling" to "General Hospital."

BEER
IS
BETTER
THAN
WOMEN
BECAUSE...

A beer bottle or beer can may "sweat", but the stuff
still tastes great.

BEER
IS
BETTER
THAN
WOMEN
BECAUSE...

A beer may cause a wet spot, but never insists you sleep on it.

BEER
IS
BETTER
THAN
WOMEN
BECAUSE...

With beers, you'll never find pantyhose in your gym bag.

A beer won't call your duck decoys "cute", giggle at your golf clothes or ask what inning it is on the 4th down.

BEER
IS
BETTER
THAN
WOMEN
BECAUSE...

A beer feels comfortable at cool temperatures and never fiddles with your thermostat.

BEER
IS
BETTER
THAN
WOMEN
BECAUSE...

A beer may cause you to use a bathroom but it will never hog it all morning.

BEER
IS
BETTER
THAN
WOMEN
BECAUSE...

A beer won't claim to be on a diet, then eat all the popcorn at the movie.

BEER
IS
BETTER
THAN
WOMEN
BECAUSE...

A beer won't mind hiding in the refrigerator
when your girlfriend comes over.

BEER
IS
BETTER
THAN
WOMEN
BECAUSE...

Beers don't want a lasting relationship.

BEER
IS
BETTER
THAN
WOMEN
BECAUSE...

Afterwards, a beer won't feel guilty, cry, propose, call her mother, your ex-wife, her therapist or take you to confession.

BEER
IS
BETTER
THAN
WOMEN
BECAUSE...

You always know when you've finished a beer. A beer can't really fake a performance.

BEER
IS
BETTER
THAN
WOMEN
BECAUSE...

A beer doesn't really care if the lights are on or off,
or if other people are watching.

BEER
IS
BETTER
THAN
WOMEN
BECAUSE...

At a singles' bar, a beer won't drop you for someone
with an accent in a flashy outfit.

BEER
IS
BETTER
THAN
WOMEN
BECAUSE...

A beer won't switch the station on your radio, return your car on empty or adjust the seat so you can't get behind the wheel. A beer will never say "It's only a small dent" or make you trade in your motorcycle for a station wagon.

BEER
IS
BETTER
THAN
WOMEN
BECAUSE...

You can enjoy a few beers on the way home and your wife will rarely complain.

BEER
IS
BETTER
THAN
WOMEN
BECAUSE...

A beer doesn't get all upset if you accidentally call it by the wrong name.

BEER
IS
BETTER
THAN
WOMEN
BECAUSE...

A beer won't beat you at arm wrestling or serve to your backhand.

BEER
IS
BETTER
THAN
WOMEN
BECAUSE...

With a beer, what you see is what you get. You'll never catch one in curlers, cold cream and a housecoat.

BEER
**IS
BETTER
THAN
WOMEN
BECAUSE...**

It's rare to get so excited about a beer that you catch something very delicate in your zipper.

BEER
IS
BETTER
THAN
WOMEN
BECAUSE...

You can make a beer last all evening or finish it right off, as you please.

BEER
IS
BETTER
THAN
WOMEN
BECAUSE...

Beers don't expect you to be faithful and never ask, "Is there another beer?" They don't care what you do with their cousins, and you never have to convince a beer you're working late.

BEER
IS
BETTER
THAN
WOMEN
BECAUSE...

A beer will never slap you with a claim for alimony,
palimony or paternity.

BEER
IS BETTER THAN WOMEN BECAUSE...

You can make a face while sipping on a beer and not blow the whole evening.

BEER
IS
BETTER
THAN
WOMEN
BECAUSE...

A beer is inexpensive to vacation with, and you can spend your holiday wherever you want.

BEER
IS
BETTER
THAN
WOMEN
BECAUSE...

You never have to take your beer shopping.

BEER
IS
BETTER
THAN
WOMEN
BECAUSE...

A good beer is never flat.

BEER
IS
BETTER
THAN
WOMEN
BECAUSE...

A beers isn't jealous of your secretary, business associates or dental hygienist.

Other books we publish are available at many fine stores. If you can't find them, send directly to us. $7.00 postpaid

2400-How To Have Sex On Your Birthday. Finding a partner, special birthday sex positions, kinky sex on your birthday and much more.

2402-Confessions From The Bathroom. There are things in this book that happen to all of us that none of us ever talk about. The Gas Station Dump, for example, or the Corn Niblet Dump, the Porta Pottie Dump and more.

2403-The Good Bonking Guide. Bonking is a great new British term for doing "you know what". Covers bonking in the dark, bonking all night long, improving your bonking, and everything else you've ever wanted to know.

2407-40 Happens. When being out of prune juice ruins your whole day and you realize anyone with the energy to do it on a weeknight must be a sex maniac.

2408-30 Happens. When you take out a lifetime membership at your health club, and you still wonder when the baby fat will finally disappear.

2409-50 Happens. When you remember when "made in Japan" meant something that didn't work, and you can't remember what you went to the top of the stairs for.

2411-The Geriatric Sex Guide. It's not his mind that needs expanding; and you're in the mood now, but by the time you're naked, you won't be!

2412-Golf Shots. What excuses to use to play through first, ways to distract your opponent, and when and where a true golfer is willing to play.

2414-60 Happens. When your kids start to look middle-aged, when software is some kind of comfortable underwear, and when your hearing is perfect if everyone would just stop mumbling.

2416-The Absolutely Worst Fart Book. The First Date Fart, The Oh My God Don't Let Me Fart Now Fart, The Lovers' Fart, The Doctor's Exam Room Fart and many more.

2417-Women Over 30 Are Better Because... Their nightmares about exams are starting to fade and their handbags can sustain life for about a week with no outside support whatsoever.

2418-9 Months In The Sac. A humorous look at pregnancy through the eyes of the baby, such as: why do pregnant women have to go to the bathroom as soon as they get to the store, and why does baby start doing aerobics when it's time to sleep?

2419-Cucumbers Are Better Than Men Because... Cucumbers are always ready when you are and cucumbers will never hear "yes, yes" when you're saying "NO, NO."

2421-Honeymoon Guide. Every IMPORTANT thing to know about the honeymoon — from The Advantages Of Undressing With The Light On (it's slightly easier to undo a bra) to What Men Want Most (being allowed to sleep right afterwards without having to talk about love).

2422-Eat Yourself Healthy. Calories only add up if the food is consumed at a table. Snacking and stand up nibbling don't count. Green M&M's are full of the same vitamins found in broccoli and lots of other useful eating information your mother never told you.

2423-Is There Sex After 40? Your wife liked you better when the bulge above your waist used to be the bulge in your trousers. You think wife-swapping means getting someone else to cook for you.

2424-Is There Sex After 50? Going to bed early just means a chance to catch up on your reading or watch a little extra t.v., and you find that you actually miss trying to make love quietly so as not to wake the children.

2425-Women Over 40 Are Better Because... Over 90 reasons why women over 40 really are better: They realize that no matter how many sit-ups and leg raises they do, they cannot recapture their 17-year-old figures—but they can find something attractive in any 21-year-old guy.

2426-Women Over 50 Are Better Because... More reasons why women over 50 are better: They will be amused if you take them parking, and they know that being alone is better than being with someone they don't like.

2427-You Know You're Over The Hill When... You tend to repeat yourself. All the stories of your youth have already bored most acquaintances several times over. Even worse, you've resigned to being slightly overweight after trying every diet that has come along in the last 15 years.

2428-Beer Is Better Than Women Because (Part II)... A beer doesn't get upset if you call it by the wrong name; and after several beers, you can roll over and go to sleep without having to talk about love.

2429-Married To A Computer. You're married to a computer if you fondle it daily, you keep in touch when you're travelling and you stare at it a lot without understanding it. You even eat most meals with it. Truly advanced computers are indistinguishable from coke machines.

2430-Is There Sex After 30? By the time you're 30, parking isn't as much fun as it was in high school. He thinks foreplay means parading around nude in front of the mirror, holding his stomach in; and she has found that the quickest way to get rid of an unwanted date is to start talking about commitment.

2431-Happy Birthday You Old Fart! You're an Old Fart when you spend less and less time between visits to a toilet, your back goes out more than you do, you tend to refer to anyone under 40 as a "kid", and you leave programming the VCR to people under 25.

2432-Big Weenies. Why some people have big weenies while other people have teenie weenies; how to find big weenies in a strange town; rating a weenie; as well as the kinds of men who possess a putz, a prong, a schwanz, a member, a rod and a wang—and more!

2433-Games You Can Play With Your Pussy. Why everyone should have a pussy; how to give a pussy a bath (grease the sides of the tub so it won't be able to claw its way out); dealing with pussy hairs (shellac it so the hairs stay right where they belong); and everything else you ever wanted to know about pussies.

2434-Sex And Marriage. What wives want out of marriage (romance, respect and a Bloomingdale's Charge Card); what husbands want out of marriage (to be left alone when watching football games and to be allowed to go to sleep after sex).

Ivory Tower Publishing Co., Inc., 125 Walnut St., P.O. Box 9132, Watertown, MA 02272-9132   Tel: (617) 923-1111